Chaos to chorus

Businesses and trust

CV Madhu

C Rajgopalachary

Real tug

- Like that Customer who has ability to be your business critics and endure opposition of your ego though it may be contained by effort because such Customer creates quick and permanent business space in innovative solutions.

Cast your costs

- To prune the global expenses due to lack of skill and clarification of business changes mapping to customer needs
- To understand what the best answer to competitors

Call your data

- Substantiate facts, hypotheses, gut, demands and challenges thrown by Customer to grow strong against other forms of opposition or support from competitors and agents

Give customers

- Professional property
- Product
- Prosperity
- Respect
- Resources for
- Innovation experiment, cooperation and understanding.

Think Customer

- Thank Customer and think like one more than expected returns or expectations of different types of stakeholders would be met but not meeting the right light that goes along Customer.

More emotional exercise

- Current scenario is no longer restricted by commercial safety of traditional values of global localisation and globalisation.

- Take efficacious emotions and thoughts towards building trust in the existentialism of Customer as star of business.

Boon or been

- One time patronage is no longer having good reason as a business touch with customers but only boom comes with strategic beam of benefits from your business success to understand what you could imagine touching improvement on user interface.

Fashionable one

- Businesses should remember not to uplift user spirits in lone fad but gathering complete experience in managing market excesses to tailor a good goal going for systematic rejuvenation of community in general.

Case study

- A middle class family in North is feeding and sheltering needy like a family, simultaneously creating brand presence of donated things without stopping by single Business and personal external contributions.

An error

- Is better than quitting customer expectations and avenues for more education of employees are better than quitting time with ideas for selling mentoring programs.

Business minds

- Mind your Customer grasp of balance between business relationship and Customer reach to understand that space not covered by books like emotion theory or true value of time.

Ufactor

- Custom services in your interest
- Not business but you alone do matter
- Universal success without you is a dream
- The I or e in business U-turn is irrelevant and error instead of internet or experience without you customer.

Main drain

- Gains directly protect Customer against other imitation offering and drain dreams not allowing advanced intelligence experiment for further loss prevention and fear of failure or fault with customers.

Example

- One man runs small brand factory which sponsors your business to SSM industry and LSE at times in return for sample distribution to the remote villages after which processing, CSR, advertising, market expansion objectives are met.

Chaos

- Bring change and adopt Customer instead of business process, plan or change itself
- Create cheers and thanks for your skill and innovation to get the complex business maze crossed
- Can contribute to current customers in better than future quitting, responding to understand future needs in current scenario.

Chaos can be

- Change osteoporosis that cripples Companies due to disobedience of stakeholders
- Current Hullabaloo After Organised Strategic medley of business changes
- Common hypothesis of approximate order status of armed knowledge that defies logic
- Competition hype adamantly opposed to submitting in front of office politics.

Chorus

- Cheers organised under Strategic stress could be a good attempt of future business ventures as integration of individual idea instead of business mob affair with your boss sheltering and not bothered to be risk-taker.

Chorus repeats

- Customer holds opportunities, results, understanding, Strategy
- Current hurdles overcome revisiting underestimated sources (huddle prevents attention to Customer focus on proximate family)
- Can hiring omit robotics usage statistics?

Business is

- Chaos when you tell Customer and chorus is customer telling you what they want
- Trip when Customer buys everything you have, chorus with customers getting everything they want from business, chaos when you sell something different from that asked by Customer

Switch

- From chorus to chaos could prick the intelligent brains to search for better future solutions and strategies for new business opportunities exploitation
- From chaotic dynamical systems to chorus could streamline the global network of users and suppliers at every loose end.

- Chaos is wave of customisation to save depth of chorus with your business mission
- Rationale behind chaos is spontaneity of xtracting dynamic capabilities behind chorus
- Chaos is chorus if you see attached patterns altering organisation, chorus is chaos if change is blocked by uniformity.

Ch - ao/ oru - s

- Beginning is toughest same for facilitating change without confusion or compromise
- Agile organisation is a good attempt to shift chaos to ordered utilisation as chorus
- End Strategy is needed for welcoming Business Customer after completion of chaos and chorus

For organisation

- Chaos is difference, chorus is uniform variation
- Chaos runs, chorus stabilizes
- Chaos is a good demon, chorus is unknown Angel
- Chaos could be change driver, chorus is preserver of business ethics.

Double standard firms

- Get the best resources lost in business chaotic change and even succumb to inertia of business chorus

- Use technology and employees alike so much as in spoiling elements of concurrence in chorus if chaos in diversification seems worst reason for customer difference.

Deal with chaos

- Find all the difference makers
- Connect with the common thread of concern
- Group the differences in skills and business changes categories
- Align well planned activities with resources to new solution for betterment of chaos.

Deal with chorus

- Too much uniformity is not a good attempt should inertia about complex innovation acceptance creep in the form of business resistance to change.
- Inductive chaos and confusion is no bad attitude towards building new ideas on different types of stakeholders.
- Train employees to enable change implementation.

Lead in chaos

- Take charge of business changes with knowledge that is going to lead others confused but confident of moving business changes ahead in avoiding penalties of rivalry and employees chaotic teams challenging goals in view of change.

Lead in chorus

- When Business complacency creeps in the global sureshot saver Strategies for well established company your role is to inform the new opportunities from the unexpected blue ocean waves of Customer deviation in business.

Common to chorus and chaos

- Company can prove that its culture is àgility
- Hi-tech ventures evolving innovation buckup ire
- Organisational structure is affected by chaos and chorus if you are not vigilant
- Strategy for chaos is observe and act, plan and act for chorus

Times

- Chorus and chaos exist forever and walk hand in hand in the different up-change and down-change of business administration and technology alignment with process aimed at making, procuring, improving, selling products for meeting customers needs at affordable prices in all times.

Factors of chorus and chaos

- Chorus taps across knowledge, chaos rests with choosing a different kind of innovative solution

- Chorus identifies the reason, chaos is spontaneity affected by effect of disorder.

- Chorus resources are needbased, chaos disturbs resources to mismanagement.

Sides of chaos - chorus

- Change is desirable but not chaos
- Chorus is not unacceptable to any management
- Inertia should be prevented from chorus being misused
- Employees should be stable and ready to say no to take the stand
- Technology should not be managed by implementation indecision.

Keys

- Chorus is tactics inputs and Strategy output
- Keywords - research, business as usual, knowledge, development

- Chaos is input on Innovation and competitors' output
- Keywords - analysis, volatility, dynamic, tasks, variables

Chords

- Chaos is chordfree to take any pitch or cacophonous tune
- Chorus chooses the chord of right progression in the global company understanding of uses
- Mix chaos in chorus for adjusting Strategy with customers' prerogative.

Connect chorus and chaos

- Chaos is like wi-fi, cordless and wireless to reach anyone from anywhere but not going anywhere from achieving a common goal if you don't interfere in time with the right plan.
- Chorus is a line of easy connection by allowing Customer interference and business resource integration of competitive completion of aims.

Use chorus and chaos

- In settling business difference between stakeholders by allowing Customer participation

- In continuing improvement or other forms of satisfaction provision by Customer

- In understanding the process deviations of Customer and economic development through technology or other forms.

Utility

- Change is the utility of chaos and process is the output of chorus with consistency as utility.

- Variation in business administration with flexibility to understand Customer in different times can grow out of strategic chaos.

- Integrity of business practices and performance can stem from Customer chorus.

Tell-tale

- Chorus should rhyme with customers but chaos should remain indoors in employees to identify different types of ideas and opportunities.
- Cheers and confusion should be accepted by your business dealing with chaos and chorus if either have to be of benefit to your business.

Market moors

- Plotting rivals to see polynomial rivalries of uncertainty in customer direction, offering Innovation, product acceptance, process excellence, operations optimisation, service delight and team inspiration
- Current customers don't have patience for real offers so add more gifts but reduce price.

Exploiting chaos in chorus

- Chaos topples business changes with goals deviating from Customer who has ability to fulfill them by competition that is ready to sell chorus of trust and care for rivalry reason as masked in customer satisfaction .

What is best?

- Chaos is no villain but some extra unrest in leading to buyer understanding supposed to be chorus in any business strategy.

- Chorus is a common contextual tone for focus on Customer worth but not value adding without various other business inputs.

- Deciding what is better could be in the given time to determine how much each is present.

Organisational structure responds

- To chaos by allowing reactions and connections between customers and employees to identify specific difference created by competitors
- To chorus by hidden interest of business with distinct goals for global community, Customer, employees because everyone has to gain for companies to get profits.

Organisational culture taps into

- Employees chorus of trust and ethics
- Resources for situational leadership with àgility
- Capabilities of resolving chaos
- Design utilising culture of chaos based on chorus and vice versa
- Structure and Strategy for managing change and stability.

Organisational skills talk

- Chords by similar response for supporting Customer attitude and interference of business mission or other changes endorsed by advanced technology that goes along new product variations in chaos on Customer worth or acceptance.

Plus minus

- Chaos stalk organisational commitment and business collaboration
- Chorus stock multiple levels cooperation with customers, companies, employees and market hierarchies
- Chaos as generating multiple ideas
- Chorus depends on one scenario.

Business Ups and downs

- Chorus cheers up crowd in pursuit of Customer
- Chaos searches for winner in cacophony of confusion with dominance
- Choosing between chaos and chorus is like decision on change or integration into modern business problem solving.

Speech

- Role of speech and communication with business stakeholders is not significant in time of chaos but chorus

- Action plan is more important and task delegation in urgency is good for handling chaos.

Deep diving

- Scarce resources can not be able to avoid loss due to chaos
- Complete knowledge can not go profitable because of chorus
- Diverse ideas may not be effective owing to chaos
- Lack of understanding can not be managed with the help of chorus.

Response transition

- Rapid response by quick change from chaos and confusion should be avoided by allowing balance of chorus with consistency of blocked or bad business cycles of inflation or other forms but surely company could choose to improve the customer experience in managing their expectations well.

Ch - vain

- Sometimes the market and community may not be able to respond or not be nice in the chaos and chorus and business developments could go in vain when representatives should be balanced with positive changes for trust by Customer commitment.

False chaos and chorus

- Company is competitive if Customer is not misled by change or order of no misunderstanding of business stakeholders in wrong interpretation of cultures in chaos and chorus because of its impact on Customer motivation to Business responsibility that may lead to failure of ventures.

Leaders

- Should be followed
- Should be balanced
- Should be inspiration
- Should be free from biases
- Should be able to pull up lessons from failure

Global network

- Chorus in global operations at different units and knowledge may be possible but not as a customer consensus unless we work by a perfect business
- Chaos is no different possibility in working world of business changes with similar response and expected results in all countries.

Innovation is chaos in chorus

- Compare old ideas and times with current ones
- Add critical check to understand what could change within your buyer
- Align above answers to bring out better needs
- The changes give customers prosperity yielding Innovation and challenges of market competitors.

Transitions are chorus

- It will appear in your business transitions that you have to deal with chaos created by Customer and employees to tackle difference in impression of business changes with knowledge, technology, experience, operations or other business modification of large impact on industry growth trajectory, globally.

Unnamed experience

- Some people are willing and ready to trust technology that goes into modern successful or bad experience of Customer in future by improving or other business changes to label the expectations of different connotation for each attention of competition value which you lose due to customers' disinterest.

Starting but not ending with customers

- The company knows how to begin a good product for users
- No company can claim success of ending with customers because they deserve to be in business always.

Bring best

- Change to pick from Customer preferences
- Resources to yield success
- Technology to receive future benefits of model

Validate best to worst

- Xtra value can come from Customer to collective business validation of market transitions in success and failure adding the learning and findings for new business solution on satisfaction of Customer chaos and managerial chorus

Carried by chaos, cared by chorus

- Business employees who are carried away by chaos can grow an appreciable success to balance it with chorus on Customer worth or acceptance decisions of long-term strategic possibilities.

Chorus and chaos exist forever

- Chorus is a common contextual tone and business development in the process
- Chaos is a good attempt to change by shifting from deviation to improvement
- Both are dependent upon technologies and employees in reducing market vagaries

Technology chorus is chaos

- As the unit of measure changes from kg to mb the system chorus is chaos of traditional employees trying to satisfy bosses with personal Ethos for grabbing a hike with technology taking that right in business now.

Uniting chaos to divide chorus

- The company should use its culture of chorus with stable Strategic concurrence for handling undecidable market changes to get chaos used to step up your internal growth efforts as competing with others strong and free.

Tick tock

- Chorus of business process is like that alarm clock warning competition in reducing chaos based tactics of wasting time by going for market mistakes, new and previous.

Essence of business

- To connect with different customers by building technology chorus in the heap of employees chaos around the appropriate approach or other business difference in culture adaptation with customers and employees.

Chicken egg situations

- Sometimes changes brought from chaos dominate employees to maintain logic based chorus and at other times business products improving solutions chorus precede the market chaos created by competitors though it is hard to understand what could come first.

The line between customers and

- Digitisation ends product innovation from authentic data restrictions
- Employees should have the market improvement or upliftment as preparation of handling chaos

Innovation option

- It's better an option than opportunity for growth in future irrespective of the product duplicate or development hassle of changing business environment into support of Innovation with exceptional experiments in supplying extremely reliable product rich in business functionalities.

Dilution of business changes

- Chaos could yield success to customer and not chorus in disruptive innovation from losing the effect of changes after a short chorus Strategy for new products made for your skill of customer delight.

Bottom line

- Resources change the process and performance of employees or machine learning
- Customer needs can grow or cut profit
- The current sales determine how the company will invest in future.

Custom Innovation

- The company knows that commodities and product innovation can grow with technology taking to customer whims in offering worth more than expected and restoration less than preparation for learning new challenge management.

Big change

- Getting started on unambiguously united project success using culture chorus and skill chaos because employees have their own ways of doing something but same ethos of essence and results yearning for success by responsibility.

Businesses bring changes

- Corporation era is not without incremental risk of chaos or chorus and business changes are wasted efforts of restoration of competition without value to buyer or corporate laws that must enrich the space of compliance.

Delving in customer direction

- Owe responsibility of returning more than expected to save Customer trust in technology when they have chaos in adjusting with culture distances before granting trust and control confidence to Business offerings.

Beneficial changes

- Chaos theory says that chorus is no longer panacea because different opinions can get better customer focus, Innovation and technology excellence of attaining the process optimisation

Choosing to be chorus

- Company could select operations or Strategy to defeat your business chaos in chorus for new business management towards building trust around Customer.

Change to exchange

- Trust in technology when leadership turns towards building market power
- Growth of employees contributing to quality social change going for systematic Customer development through coexistence of encouraging environmental support and challenges.

Value change

- Business change through transitioning from chaos to ordered utilisation of capabilities and chorus to chaos could give good reason that adds new value for Customer by taking community value in consideration of corporate objectives

Chorus changes

- Market trends and patterns that guide business solution for your progress through stable times in the industry growth or decline could give customers prosperity by allowing good transformation in business globally.

Etching process

- Etching process and technology excellence of attaining unambiguous innovation and excellence by running operations for Customer importance to get new impact of market challenge could give good learning experience.

Bait of chorus and chaos

- Current customers can easily find more avenues for business development of competitors and throw changes brought by the chaos
- Technology can get worse side of failure or fault with your customer to eliminate any sure shot success brought by bait of chorus.

Value of consistency change

- The changes that are driving companies at restorating consistency add critical analysis that is precious for remote gathering of value information on enhancing use of Technologies.

Looking for new change

- Chorus may be more of the change in favour of Customer as your quick business future by overcoming past market hurdles, blunders and failure with ventures around social networks but not without incremental skill perfection or new chaos in market players that is too a change in deriving opportunities for growth.

Addressing

- Chaos asks for resonance with customer cultural distance, employee innovation, product features or your new competitive change to form chorus in giving more clarity by positivism for your skill, business, Customers.

Unite change, chorus

- Alignment of deviation in business chorus to get the right view of change movements in the business chaos can implement useful projects on prevention of flaws due to market volatility and Customer uncertainty of exact needs.

Differentiate chaos and chorus

- The changes in business should consider effects of chaos or chorus in disruptive innovation and technology excellence by running along new product Strategy or market intelligence of deriving solutions beyond Customer expectations.

Minting change

- Monitor your business credibility in customer satisfaction by providing change to check your user experiences but not as guide for agile tactics, àgility should be your independent best without resting on Customer.

Rolling chorus

- Discover chorus in changing business dynamics or Customer needs as continuous rotation of the product management efforts of restoration between customers and employees to get new impact of business effort without departing from Customer trust.

Correct your business

- To be part of changes with knowledge that is becoming of Customer chorus
- To connect in culture of chaos based in business etiquette feeding trust by which we have a good choice of business solution for betterment of Customer service.

International balance

- The changes that you should get are those of business capabilities as chorus to be assisted by chaos and chaos in adjusting to chorus because they deserve equal importance to be leader of international operations.

From Customer

- To employees is a good journey attaching many resources and needs
- To investors is not just consensus on the path of Innovation but including Business cause for change within your buyer esteem to get multiple upticks.

To customer

- First before the need is fixed, give your best business time.
- Next during the process of establishing offer with ready solutions give good reason to buy.
- Then after that Offering is not satisfying customer give them your response, resources and services to provide true delight.

Need no

- Chaos theory needs more than ideas for not taking losses due to man-made reason that try to manage difference in Strategy
- Chorus in business globally can grow trained user values and doesn't need products or services in order for Customer retention

Tables

- Chaos multiply resources and benefits when capabilities are not scattered in unproductive directions

- Chorus multiply for your application increasing international quality by advanced customisation inviting basis of business changes.

More than modern trend

- Chaos is not just a modern business development but some assurance that employees are not hesitating to think free for Innovation
- Chorus is not managed but emerges as your quick response in competitive strategy.

Twin effects

- Chorus and chaos could help working on business and Customer goals at the same time
- Both Cs could close on Customer worth or Business efforts at the right measure

Ring bell

- When market is innovative and business changes are not going for chorus
- When Customers could not generate chaos in market for guidance on how to use signals from competition.

Dramas of market

- Competition is now slowly labelled as uninformed
- High bidder is not winner but Business egoist
- Customer is in process of establishing superiority by behaviour or culture stolen from the others.

Best response

- In chaos, run on their decision assessment for new business opportunity in the fastest growing Customer

- In chorus, adapt to new perspective or other business changes for your customer cooperation.

Last but not lost

- Chaotic teams and discipline of chorus should be balanced with positive agreement of Customer demands for dynamic agility and strength of making leadership advantages by allowing advanced business intelligence to meddle with the market signals.